a ritual of drowning

TABOR SARAH BOOKS   Oakland : Palo Alto

A RITUAL
OF
DROWNING

poems of love and mourning

Teya Schaffer

Tabor Sarah Books
367 50th Street
Oakland, CA 94609

Text fonts Classical Garamond and Aldine401

Publisher's Cataloging-in-Publication Data
Schaffer, Teya, 1948-
    A Ritual of Drowning: poems of love and mourning/
Teya Schaffer – 1st ed.

    I. Title
811.54
ISBN 0-935079-18-1

dedicated to the memory of

Jackie Winnow

activist for justice
and lover of cats

and to

Richard Lipperman and
T. Asher Adar Schaffer

for being there

Contents

Closure   3

part one

August   7

A Valentine   8

Seasons   10

The New Year   11

Disbelief   16

Afterimage   18

Saturday   19

Changeling   20

Resting Place   21

Homesick   22

Symptoms   23

Family Ties   24

Two Widows   25

Bones   26

What Makes the Story   28

Faith   29

When Your Ghost   30

Anniversary   32

July Diary   35

Widow Interviewed   38

Content, Language, Poem   39

Stepping Off the Curb   41

part two

In the Garden   45

for the friends of Barbara Schmoller   46

For Shem's Mother   47

Car Art   50

A Ritual of Drowning   51

Acknowledgements
Author's Note

a ritual of drowning

Closure

i

It is not like drowning any more:
your life no longer a silent film
flickering before my eyes.
No, now you are wrapped like a holy text
over arm and forehead, enscrolled
on the doorposts of my house,
a commandment of remembrance.

ii

I am not done.
I am not finished missing you.
How could memory forget its creator?
the ungiven future would have found us
seeking still the persuasive truths
which show the beloved her beauty;
how could memory forget its purpose?

iii

First I loved you
true and well.
You loved me like a tree:
canopy and root.
In those days I could speak your name
in all the public places.

When you were dying
your name became a wreath
on my brow, marking me
as more than I was;
people took your name from my lips
and poured it burning into my ears.
You were a burning crown
and now are ash:
a future bereft of prediction
a silence caught in the teeth.

iv

your name was Jackie
when you mocked my vanities
my heart was comforted
when you nested your fears in my heart
my courage was sufficient
when you broke my heart with refusal
I still was whole
when my failings tripped your strength
your love was not diminished
what if death is unceasing
there are other things
which last as long

part one

August

When dark follows heat
into the house, and sweat
rests before drying on our skin
my child makes stealthy rounds,
closing windows.
We haven't said
Death comes a thief
only the honest words
cancer metastases.
He watches the night,
builds scarecrows against someone
moving in the field.

A Valentine

She grows thin,
wears loss like the necklace of her collarbone.
Every day another goodbye
announced by pain.

We exhaust in tandem.
She withdraws from the dramas of the healthy
I withdraw from her, losing jealousy;
the time she gives to others
has become my rest.
In half-sleep I remember
what held us
the pull of gravity
full moon on water
the light
palms filled with flesh, hip and belly,
the far reach of our arms
the way our return to shore was guaranteed.
The body does not rest.
I purchase her birthday gift wondering
how soon I'll wear it.
Her Valentine's Day card burns my fingers:
When this you see/Remember me.

Atheists, we enter sacred space
with only our bodies to hold the mortal soul;
we enter death's culvert naked
skin scraped raw by the narrowing walls
trading off the task of torchbearer.
Soon the path will refuse me
soon the dissolution of heart
and my soulless return
but now we are the work of our bodies
dying and tending.
She catches me with her glance,
interrupts the swabbing of a catheter port
or the removal of an emesis basin,
to hold us
  it is like the breath of sleepers
  drawing each other in through slightly parted lips,
  it is like breathing
  it is like a cell carrying oxygen to the furthest need
  and returning for more,
  it is like the talk of love and the sacrifices made,
  but more like walking and the rhythms of that walk
  it is the road home in moonlight

then we continue
with our work.

Seasons

Flowers on a bush
roses, my son calls them, for their color,
their many petals, but they are something else.
I do not know their name. In the right season
I sweep the debris of growth from our front steps;
underneath the rosy petals it is damp,
and dangerous
to careless walkers.

Each season is appropriate
although calendars are collected against it;
frost comes early, snow stays late—
we demand spring but spring is here
on our cold cheeks.

The New Year

i

Conveniently our street ends in the cemetery where we
used to take the baby in his stroller, bicyclists and joggers
more common than mourners. We make an appointment,
"pre-need." Learn prices and locales. The number of
people allowed in each plot varies with terrain and
container, casket or urn. Stones must lie flat. We are
already out of our bodies just being there.

At least the quarrel is behind us, of where to rest in
perpetual care. Generic ground spreads near the entrance.
The old Jewish section is lovely but filled; the new one,
treeless as a subdivision, is a long mile uphill. She refuses to
be buried "in a ghetto." I won't lie "among strangers."
First going gets first dibs; I give way and see her desire:
that there be passersby to read her name.

ii

She prepares for her death with a to-do list, a lined yellow
pad at the ready. We research mortuaries because it's our
habit to know, to care, our questions a parody of the
search for health. Who will touch her body? How long can
it stay at home? We want refrigeration, not embalming. I
go without her to the showroom. "Not 'cheap,'" a wincing
salesperson corrects me, "'inexpensive.'" Either way I

choose her box; consult at home, "lined or not?" At Albert Brown's I'm warned away from washing her myself— death's not pretty, the consultant says. So I go with Chapel of the Chimes. How do I go on, walking down the street, buying the child his dinner? From her bed she hands me the yellow tablet: a penciled rectangle, name, dates, beloved.

iii

The hidden businesses are revealed. Goodbye to the local pharmacy and its line of caregivers buying Tylenol with codeine and Ensure. On to the farther one, smaller and darker, which sells morphine. In come the supplies, the rail for the toilet, the i.v. pole and its bags of saline. Out goes our mattress in the arms of a stranger returning with a cot and a hospital bed. We sit in the midst, with a hospice nurse disappointed by our talk of nausea when she'd hoped for our souls. In the quieter hours we keep to two rooms, quietly dying, quietly stitching a rose.

iv

Her death reads like a book, the labored and infrequent breaths pages from a year of study; friends and family pose in quiet vignettes. The child comes to sit in my lap, his hands colder than hers; then he leaves with an uncle. The cats follow their needs, one curls by her face, the other on a high shelf ready to thump down with her last breath. Outside the window and two floors below, a band is

playing for some undeclared holiday, a merchants'
celebration. In between her rattling sounds, rise
unmistakable bars of "When the Saints Come Marching
In." The telephone rings, someone wants to know if she's
still here. The cat comes down.

v

I ask for privacy. I close the door; pull back the blanket;
remove the catheter. Join you. The press of my body
releases a final sigh from yours. My fingers discover the
you without you, greeting and leaving your toes and the
spaces between your toes, right foot and left, ankle and
shin, the manner of your walk, knee and thigh, the
memory of fat, hip and buttocks, my palm mating the
curve of pubic bone hello goodbye the skin of your
abdomen, the shadows beneath your breasts, your breasts
and the breast which betrayed us hello goodbye scars the
hollow of your collarbone the sparse hairs beneath your
arm the inside of your elbow the stilled veins the narrow
wrist the fit of our hands the turn of my face into your
neck. This is the moment we have waited for; I won't
leave it for years.

vi

Wash cloths, basin. Someone asks "shampoo?" three say
"no need." Her dying was clean, her body not impure,
still we understand: before going into the dirt she must
be touched by water. Soft terry barely damp, a murmur

13

of direction as we lift and lower; mother, sister, friend, spouse, tenderly, thoroughly, smoothing our way over her going. Her eyes half-open, as if this is something she would like to see.

vii

I cross the threshold, carrying her like a bird in my mouth; recognize the shapes of people as I move towards an empty room. Marvelous the stillness of their language, the sympathy in their distance, as if they too feel the concussed air rippling between us. A way is being made for the widow, on its quiet I place my feet.

viii

There are no Sunday gravediggers. Consternation and phone calls. Jews bury their dead on the following day unless that day is forbidden for mourning. Her friends get busy: she was a person of connections, maybe there are strings to pull. Her sister asks if the photographs, brought too late for viewing, can be buried with her. A friend offers stones. They are coming for her body. We pull crayon drawings off the refrigerator, a ribbon rose from the dresser—don't be lonely, don't forget us, here's something for the journey we don't believe you take.

I flee when the doorbell rings, return, after her body's gone, with new wisdom: she is dead, she can wait until

Monday. Monday is the New Year, a forbidden day, but I
don't care. We never cared for rituals we couldn't use.

ix

All I am asked to do is breathe. Her mother offers gin. Her
sister a sleeping pill. They are good gifts. In the morning
they bring me tea and toast. We blame our exhaustion on
the visitors and look forward to their return. It is right and
good, this ingathering of mourners to verify a loss, their
offerings of food. I remove the flower someone has placed
on her pillow, try not to wince when someone sits on
her bed.

x

Tomorrow we go to the cemetery. Tonight it is erev Rosh
Hashanah. I prepare apples and honey, share with my son
the sweetness of life. My tongue cradles the bird in my
mouth, tells her the new year will never come.

Disbelief

I wake up amazed by my cheerfulness,
so glad of the sun,
although I know you are dead.
I go through the subsiding day
only slightly stunned by your absence,
its thoroughness.
On the street I find myself
one universe over
from the one I've known,
wish for an armband
to signify the journey.

I know you are dead.
The elementary school posts your obituary.
The hospital in a flurry of housecleaning
sends daily bills for blood drawn a year ago.
The red glass which held a seven-day candle
sits empty on my son's dresser.
The photographs meant to hold you
flatten into strangers.
In a drawer, the diminishing ratio of
neatly folded socks to knotted pairs
reveals the change in wearer.

I open another drawer
and another.
I close the drawers
and look in the closet
and in another.
I open kitchen cabinets.
I wander in and out of rooms.
At each window, an empty view.

I haven't seen your face outside a dream.
I never rise to the bait of a telephone ringing.
I take my longing to the street
peering in shop windows, retracing our steps.
Even the cemetery can not persuade me;
on my way home I see the mail truck
and my steps quicken.
You have never been away so long
without writing.

Afterimage

absence : a flash

spots before the eyes
I see her
I see her

bruises from trying to walk
when I can't
see anything else

Saturday

Consistent as roadside markers in headlights
when white lines of highway blur with speed
every Saturday you die

All of Thursday the calendar called two months dead
but Thursdays don't speak of you so
all day I looked at seven, the seventh of the month
but that didn't resonate either all day
but on Friday it's too round-the-curve close and

There's that orange reflector.
Check the clock: yes now
you have stopped breathing   and now
the white of your eye is sinking and
now   you're getting into a car
and driving away

Changeling

Once upon a time,
when you still lived,
Grief hid in the back
of the closet,
a bogeyman
biding his time.
The narrow space
smelled of dirt and insects;
his dank breath
caught in the sleeves of my shirts,
creeping cold up my arms.

Now Grief takes an elfin turn.
Wearing the shape of your body,
she tells stories
in your voice
of how it used to be.
Her breath counterpoint
to mine, we walk
with hip riding against hip
in the old joining.
Enchanted, I take her
to bed.

Resting Place

I make your bed with shears cutting the grass, arranging pebbles and flowers to edge the stone pillow. You are not beneath the level rock: the press-wood box begins several inches downhill. I try to remember this when I touch the grass: where your head might be and where your feet.

Some days I am only hands and knees squatting to an indifferent task, clipping clipping; other days I am curator of your museum: grave or me the final artifact. I step back critically and try for the stranger's glance—will this display attract a reading of your name?

The dried flowers stand up purple-headed. The tending finished, my empty hand reaches through the grass. Ants are busy everywhere, and silence.

Some nights I dream my next-best dream: you mumble from your blanket-burrow how tired you are, and reach a hand for mine before sleeping.

Homesick

like nightime in an unfamiliar bed,
the sheets stay stiff to the body
and it's not crickets outside but cars or
it's not cars but raccoons—something
tearing the background away
so sleep has to take a different route.

Symptoms

The twitch in my eyelid
was a side effect of your chemo treatments.
The revelation of your lung's disease
became a small circle of baldness
shining on the side of my head.
As you lost time, I lost perspective:
my wallet disappeared in the car;
the car bereft of guidance
caught on curbs.
Finally a blow to the inner ear:
unhinged from past and future
I reeled in death's eternal present.
Still I never lost my appetite.
My tongue desired cookies,
cakes, puddings,
the sweetness of apples
and honey,
even when the parking spaces narrowed
and I circled the lots
unable to stop searching
or stop.

Family Ties

Mother-in-law:
your sisters, your husband
are they all buried on Long Island?
Do you light yahrzeit candles in Miami
and do they come like moths the whole long way?
I search the cemetery ground for your daughter
flowers like a divining rod
pull down to her grave.

Two Widows

Tonight another woman unfolds "widow"
with her tongue, rolls it in the suddenly
cavernous gape of her mouth.
In the well of her throat a name
is drowning; her own breaths
dull and shallow, as if the air held
bad news.

I will come before the infinite shock
turns to hours and days,
bringing the black crepe,
the rituals which do no harm,
my unplumbed throat.
Leaning in close, as for confidences,
I'll keep my own counsel
and she won't blame me later,
when the news is seized in her teeth
and her ears burn with absence,
for what I couldn't say
her name is leaving the common tongue
listen.

Bones

Without warning
her name disappears.
People shy
from the syllables
which formed her.
Somewhere,
in another tongue,
people are spreading their
dead in the branches of trees.
In another country
they create huge jars
for fermenting rice wine, and others
for decomposing relatives.
There are communal ceremonies
for disinterment: remains are
unearthed, rearranged, buried
again. I think of these people
as I sit alone cleaning her bones.

I feel her weight on the mattress at night,
in the morning hear her voice call from the kitchen
with an offer of fruit. She stands next to me,
unreflected in the mirror.
I entered the grave at night
returned with two hundred and six bones.

I clean them in sand.

My son meets me here where death
is not a journey, mourning not a path,
drawn and repelled by my work.
He stays for a chorus of "the worms
crawl in, the worms crawl out"
before moving away.

If I say this small shape
is the hyoid, in life the only bone
unconnected to any other, a support
for her voice, and that the minimus
where she wore our ring, will I have said
anything?
I say "her" bones, as if she
could claim them. I call "come back
no questions asked—I will believe
anything." The bones remain bones.

Some people
split them open and eat the marrow.
I gather them on a blanket,
make a bundle, hoist it over my shoulder;
not heavy, just awkward, an adjustment.
I walk with the muffled click and clack of her bones
knocking along my ribs and spine, listening
for her name.

What Makes the Story

What makes the story of my lover's death interesting is the
delivery of the pills, how she said "death" and mimed
swallowing because she was losing words and needed to
know delivery was at hand. Also the social embarrassment
the day before when I'd asked her: should I get them?
because there's something so unseemly in asking the
departing if they want a push so I didn't hear her answer
quite and had to stumble through it again so she rolled
her eyes at her mother saying "Teya can be so slow
sometimes," and back to me saying "Yes, I'm saying yes."
And then the long list of who should come and say
goodbye, and the setting of the date and the oh dear what
if she wakes up Saturday morning and doesn't remember
that this is the day or can't say she remembers even though
we just got this clear must I remind her and isn't that rude?
but fortunately she says "Let's get this show on the road"
and her sister and I giggle emptying capsules into tea and
when I lift the cup to her mouth I murmur encouragements
"there you go, that's good, almost done," and when she's
done we all say "L'chaim," except for her.

Faith

Now that you are dead
who will keep bleak faith with me?
who staunch my soul against heretical
whimsy? Everywhere they raise you
perched on cloud or bardo
casting downward glances
to my pain. Happy! they say
you and the others gone before
smile, while I strain through time
for the comfort of you alive
and never so cruel as that.

When Your Ghost

When your ghost appears

my hands cup the air,
my palms prickle, recognizing the weight that fills them,
my toes curl and uncurl, ready to leave for foreign places;
my vertebrae straighten.
Your body, boneless as a newborn's, shifts to my shape,
fills my hollows, presses into every empty space,
knows me.

The hairs on my arm rise with pleasure.

To resuscitate the drowned, lifeguards were trained
to compress and release the chest;
my heart knows your touch and resumes beating.

You appear neither clothed nor naked;
your eyes are without face, scattering light
as oceans do the sun.
Fearful of where you'll leave me, memory doubts
the angle at which our eyes meet, I say
"Your irises never held so much green."
They hold our very best days, our very best selves...

...I would not look away

but you pour yourself like air into my empty lungs
where spikes of grief snag each breath,
you enter the bloodstream inscribing yourself
on veins and arteries
and behind my eyes—
tears rush as if I'd never known weeping
or its ending;
no more revived, I am never-drowned still-drowning
rocked in the skin of myself

when your ghost disappears
I see its absence.

Anniversary

You return from I-don't-ask-where,
we kiss for an eternity
but you can't stay long.
You return from the coast,
no apologies for not calling sooner.
We're still partners;
we've broken up.
You've forgotten that you're dead
and I don't remind you.
I go down stairs, down ramps, down south
on clandestine missions of rescue—
your name changes, your sex changes,
but it is always you
and I always fail.
I wake in the middle of the night
in cold terror: you are dead
and I've forgotten to cry.

I braid the nights' dreams into my hair.
I twist my grief into a lock of spine,
and swallow your taste of coffee
with my breakfast.
Getting into the car
I look for your smile, and find
the get-away grin of a road trip,

vacation memories fill the morning commute.
I create you daily,
still your life narrows.

Alone at work
I set your name spinning on the air,
and you dance
you shimmy between the coffeepot
and the water heater, leaning forward
to give me a whiff of deep cleavage,
turning 'round to remind me of your flat ass,
your fingers still slick from all the days
spent autographing my cunt, and your lips
in their after-sex satisfaction—
all afternoon I carry you like a fire

but you cool on my sheets
your eyes sinking back into their sockets.

Even photographs turn on me,
replacing memory with fact.
When I hold you up to the living
you disappear; your life of snap and flare
an echo of light on the wall,
not your shade but my shadow.
I search my diary for a record of time
but it is all dreams and longing,
a story beginning and ending in "once."

The mirror reflects on my narrowed
eyes, the thinning of my lips, time happens
without you, with you nothing happens
to me.
The candle flickers in its glass.
If you can't stay,
go.

July Diary

Ants in the sink, Olympics on tv. The adolescent away and unchaperoned. A visit to the graveyard to confirm a crime. A book.

Mercedes de Acosta loved Greta Garbo who lost her American earnings in a bank failure 1930s. Mercedes did not kill ants.

My favorite lesbian moment of the Olympics was a kiss that didn't happen.

The crime was not a poetic allusion to death: every June I plant a rainbow flag by the headstone, and an anonymous yet faithful enemy breaks the staff and rips the cloth; I retrieve the pieces in July.

When he returns safely from being away and unchaperoned for three days and two nights, the adolescent will go to his girlfriend's house and put on makeup before the evening's concert.

The U.S. women gymnasts hug as directed by their coaches; the Russian men kiss so sweetly I want a replay; and the Ukrainian—she and her girlfriend do it like the movies. One is radiant from a perfect routine, the other comes forward to embrace her; we see through the camera's lens a definition of "barely suppressed": these teenagers touching, moving together as if to, but if they did? the electricity fills the screen and my living room. They hold each other passionately apart.

I pretend I am not killing ants while washing dishes, vigorously splashing water out of cups. After the drain empties, tiny bodies stick to the sides, some dead, some still wriggling.

Marlene Dietrich sent de Acosta too many flowers. Mercedes was personally unaffected by the Depression but as a personality she was often suicidally sad. She believed in karma and was extremely wealthy.

My lover died earlier than is expected for American women born in 1947, and did not believe in karma. I am afraid to learn how much my son has forgotten of her. Did I remember to tell him that when we met she still liked an occasional toke?

It is illegal in many places to smoke marijuana, to crossdress, to name one's lover, to deface a grave. Four criminal young men drove a car into my car while I was in it. It was nothing personal but they laughed before running away so I wish them ill.

I recuperate in bed, reading Mercedes' autobiography.
Afraid to be alone, I let my son go away. The ants thin,
regroup, surround the sink again. The female swimmers
shave their pubic hairs so completely I am embarrassed.
The curl in my lover's hair has also vanished.

Widow Interviewed
after six years

a young voice on the phone
thanks me for my time
my willingness to give her quotes
"It must be so hard to talk about,"
she says. I laugh
warmly
from the hearth
where you dance
like a flame licking wood
like a spark flying outside
the perimeter of safety
the fire wall
my heart.

I try to describe
one arc: a hiss of sap
from green wood, a spit
of firefly and darkness.
If allowed
I would talk
all day   the pleasure
you
aflame.

Content, Language, Poem

"It's not the content but the language,"
I protest, sweaty from wrestling a poem
into imperfect form.
"I know this stuff. I've said it out loud
more than once, over many years."
I imagine my listeners are…forbearing.

It is always the content;
a poorly-recognized truth turns shield up
against the natural force of poetry,
trips into the conversation
on a slip of tongue.
"When *I* was dying," I tell them
and go on talking as if we hadn't heard
this confusion of pronoun.
I want to say *she was dying*.
I never wanted to say it.
Even when it passed my lips,
it went unsaid.

I am only sister to the I
who shared a death
and died.
The past
sits on my tongue

sure as any ghost of its rights.
They want my words, that *she*, that *I*.
They want this work, this shoulder
to the shovel digging, and my reward:
bones. *Skeletons.* A fool's job
to stand at poem's end in pain.

This is half a lie.

I enter memory cautiously,
ever the child at poolside,
slowly testing temperature,
buoyancy.
At the deep end a poem surfaces.
This is what I could have:
for the length of one unbreathing dive
embodiment
—my self alive in her beating heart—
the gasp of air
—she lives! she dies!—

then
(if I don't shiver in the cooling air
or, shivering, find my warmth)
a poem.

Stepping Off the Curb

The dead are not in our hearts.
We call their names out loud
precisely because they are not there.
On the street, in public places,
our lips move visibly as we walk
and the words
whisper.

We call to them first
with the sigh of their proper names
and then, the new affections
which loss has taught us:
heart's desire, heart's ache.
While walking
whispering
the light becomes
more yellow,
something breathing with memory
charges the air
a single note held off key
or *sawdust, its bright incense*
—the dead are with us—
bringing the song itself
and a forgotten glance well met
above a dusted floor.

Eagerly, we reply with all
that has gone on, everything
the trouble with the sink,
the joke at work, what it's been like
sitting in the dark; our restless days
find anchor.

We are grieved
but not foolish.
This corner, how long
have we been standing here?
We stuff the dead
into pants pockets:
they jingle in our hands
with coins and keys;
or we draw them into our mouths:
they'll call their names out in our sleep.
Stepping off the curb, they disappear like ghosts
in the changing light; we cross the street,
thinking of rain and dinner.

part two

In the Garden

In this garden,
the branches of one tree pass through
the arms of another, creating a hybrid
of blossoms: yellow and upward, white and heavy.
Below, orange nasturtium surround something green
which shouldn't be there in the first place,
threatening as it does to grow bark. Cactus flowers
catch the laundry limp on the line, while an unknown
plant, content til now inside its patio boundaries,
sends naked tendrils into the air, hoping for tree
(I shift my lounge-chair vantage beyond its current range).
Ivy on its march up the wall engulfs the telephone box.
Blackberry vines hide the cement, and foxtails
—spiky, clinging things—threaten to leave their stalks
for other transport: the cat, or my pants' leg.
Overhead the sun and a black helicopter beat down.
A fig tree pushes its way between fence slats,
preventing the gate from closing;
everything green and bright
suggests I leave.

for the friends of Barbara Schmoller

Each breath leaves the body
even the last   moves towards another mouth
This taste   birch bark tea   Barbara
hears us calling through her death
and returns   amazing all
with her focusing eyes
These three days she is returning
smiles, a little bit of language,
helped to sit, she stands   shuffles
each bare foot a lesson for the one behind
May we hope?
or only say we loveyouloveyoulove
will missyoumissyoumiss and here
Here. Another Noon.
Another Evening Meal. Take it,
I have cooled it with my breath.

For Shem's Mother

O heart
the Himalayas turned topsy turvy,
their heights now depths of grieving;
what words could sound this chasm?
  It is your son's birthday
  and he is one year buried.
The air hangs motionless beside your face

a kiss would not disturb it nor a sigh:
we plant one on either cheek,
we who feed the children's breath with our own
—first for their survival and then,
then we continue, past lullabies and years,
it is a definition:
mothers breathe a double passage,
for well or ill, unavoidable
like seeing death on the curbstone
—the car swerving/stalling/skidding—
watching accidents before they happen
even when they never;
like seeing love, the shining fruit, a bite
in our child's mouth, radiant through the cheeks,
and swallowing the knowledge they can't learn from us;
our diaphragms moving as they pass through schools and

jobs and jails, friends and lovers,
sickness, health.

Are we clever? are we good? do they rise and call us
household deities, still curled on their chests, purring
stealing their dreams away?
Benign or evil, willy-nilly
a breath on the cheek of the slumbering man,
the rising daughter,
everywhere mother—

if only this were magic and not a definition
if only bearing life were magic and not nature
if only letting them go insured their going on
if only knowing danger wove a charm
if only looking ahead changed the future
if only traveling a hard road yielded an easier one
if only moments could be recalled, held up, turned over
in the sun so the steps which led to steps fell
on a different path
if only this rising and falling
if only this silent lift and fall
if only

even the wind screamed,
the mountain freed sound
as it tore from itself
root and rock

groaning protest
before meeting his bones
—did he think the voice yours?
You were only a breath upon his glazing eyes

and now it is returned:
the air of the world close and still
filling your lungs with all you know of him,
a weight on the ribs, a cloak of warning—
we grab our breath before holding you close.

Car Art

(the story of Jewel Box and her creator can
be found in *Wild Wheels* by Harrod Blank)

Jay Battenfield, chronicler of grief, affixes rings, bracelets,
pearls, rubies, necklaces (the gifts he gave her, the baubles
she treasured), seals them in pattern, in gaudy beauty, on a
car. Meticulous mourning sets the story of each diamond
precisely where it needs to be: hood, roof, hubcap, every
inch is covered and he knows where each memory rests,
the car becoming something real like their love.

Jay Battenfield, aging white man of Amarillo, Texas, your
driver-side door glitters in red and white with stars on a
field of blue: you are no one I would feel safe knowing and
your car could feed many. Who knows what Jean would
say if the anonymous truck hadn't sucked her, and her car,
under? Your car is hard in its pain: she will never wear
these again/no one will ever wear them again.

Jay Battenfield, healing the world like a poet, displays his
heart on a 1960 Corvair so we can see what is missing: that
which gives value to rubies. He receives the grieving
citizens of Amarillo, and what we carry—the wedding
bands and bangles our dead abandoned—he sets in place.
More. He remembers on fender and fin their worth.

A Ritual of Drowning

Some drown in the ocean and some in the river, some drown in ponds, or lakes or creeks. Some die on their way to drowning, dashed against rocks. Some die startled and some die ready. The ones who are ready come to our sea.

The ritual of drowning for those who are ready is not the ritual of drowning for the suicide, the accident, the murder, is not the ritual for the careless, the unguarded young, the invalid unable to escape a flood. There are rituals for these but it is not the ritual of drowning for those who are ready.

They come alone sometimes but more often attended, the ready. Their belovéds come: mates, family, friends, they come trailing doubts and longing but discreetly, tying them to belt fringe, tucking them into sock cuffs. Those who are ready for the ritual of drowning have faint life in their bodies, can no longer be held by doubt or desire. Some come walking, more are carried, to the lip of our sea.

Those who are ready for the ritual of drowning sometimes come alone but often are attended. The death barge accepts only one or two or three to serve them. It sails out slowly and quickly, quickly lost to the ones on shore, slowly to we who have been waiting; to the one who is ready, and the belovéds, the barge floats in no time. I raise myself in the water, water rushing down my long hair, air raising my nipples, tail thrashing the sea to thrust me high into their sight. It is part of the ritual and so I do it, but the belovéds look only at the ready, and the ready look at the sea.

I settle lower in the water. The barge drifts near, the sea slap-slaps its side. No words are spoken on the barge; there is no music; these are the ready who have scant life left in them. I lift up the cup brimming with sea. A belovéd receives it. Those who are ready drink, and are lowered into my arms.

I carry the drowning to their death at the bottom of this sea. Now there can be singing and so I sing them through their drowning, mermaid songs of no significance. They relax and let float out of their bodies visions of their life on the land. They sigh and sink, sigh and sink, out of my arms to the sea floor, ready to become bones.

The death barge awaits my surfacing, no cup, no body, a sober neutrality upon my face. When the ritual is done correctly, the survivors bow, and turn grieving back to land. When it is done correctly, they sail on the barge back to shore. Sometimes, sometimes, a belovéd hears something in the slap of water on the boat's side. Sometimes, watching for the mermaid's return, a belovéd sees something that is not seaweed twining in the mermaid's hair. When the life the dead has lived on land rises visible to a human eye, the ritual hesitates. Most belovéds then turn, grieving, to land. And others, seeing in each wave their love, become mermaids.

Acknowledgements

From the Berkeley Women's Center writing workshops of the 1970s, through the East Bay Jewish Lesbian Writers Group of the '80s, and Oregon's Flight of the Mind in the '90s, my work has been encouraged and shaped by gatherings of women dedicated to the pursuit of the right word. My thanks to all, and especially to the members of my current writing group: Susan Dambroff, Kim Innes, Chris Kammler, Helen Mayer, Mary Carol Randall, Margaret Thalhuber, and Chana Wilson for their critiques and wit.

Individual women offered much needed literary and/or technical support in the manuscript's final stages. Thanks to Elana Dykewoman, Megan Hughes, Keiko Lane, Judith Masur and Patti Schaffer.

Susan Liroff volunteered her expertise in computers and graphic design, patiently bringing me from ignorance to page one and beyond. Her generous gifts of enthusiasm and time made a daunting task not only approachable but possible.

I am indebted, most of all, to Maggie Rochlin, who in 1978 said "Let's try a writing workshop" and has been giving me good editorial advice ever since. From her support in my early grief to her participation in design decisions, Maggie's insights are woven into these pages.

Author's Note

Jackie Winnow died on September 7, 1991. On September 9th, the San Francisco Board of Supervisors adjourned its regular meeting in honor of her life.

Jackie had an activist's heart, always looking for the work which needed to be done, never questioning that she had a responsibility to do it. We met while organizing the 1982 Jewish Feminist Conference in San Francisco: she was there to do her part and I was there to find a lover. We were both successful.

She had graduated summa cum laude in Women's Studies from S.F. State University and was the first Coordinator of the Lesbian/Gay and Aids Unit of the S.F. Human Rights Commission. In response to her own diagnosis of cancer, Jackie founded the Women's Cancer Resource Center in 1986, the first organization of its kind in the nation. As her way of acknowledging the many activists whose work is never publicly honored, Jackie asked that nothing be named for her after her death.

Jackie loved the words "feminist" and "lesbian," enjoyed good coffee, "I Love Lucy," and buying from clothes catalogs. She died at the age of 44, leaving one child, two cats, many friends, relatives, and the author to treasure her memory.

To Order *A RITUAL OF DROWNING*

Books ordered _____ x $8.95   = _____

CA residents add $.74 sales tax per copy   = _____

Postage and Handling $1.50 first copy   = _____
           each additional copy $.50   = _____

                     Total   = _____

Discount of 20% offered on orders of 5 or more

Name _____

Address_____

City_____State_____Zip_____

Make checks or money order payable to

     Tabor Sarah Books
     367 50th Street
     Oakland, CA 94609